Published By Adam Gilbin

@ Gene Davidson

Carnivore Diet: A Beginner's Guide for Optimum Health and Fitness With the Carnivore Diet

All Right RESERVED

ISBN 978-1-990666-65-0

TABLE OF CONTENTS

Cajun-Spiced Chicken Livers With Bacon And Onion 1

Scotch Turkey Eggs 4

Lobster Tails With Animal Butter 6

Keto Mushroom Omelet 8

Instant Pot Steamed Crab Legs 10

Spice-Rubbed Bison Tenderloin 11

Carnivore Stroganoff 13

Carnivore Cake 14

Easy Almond Crusted Fish Recipe 16

Baked Salmon 19

Carnivore Waffles 20

Carnivore Taco Pie 22

Vietnamese Lamb 24

Seared Bacon Burgers 26

Savory Baked Chicken Thighs 27

Keto Quesadillas 29

Mesquite Garlic Trout 32

Beef Patties With Onion Gravy 34

Lemon Carnivore Cheesecake 36

Easy Salt And Pepper King Fish Recipe 40

Baked H2 Y & Spice Chicken 42

Carnivore Frittata 44

Carnivore Cake 46

Crab Stuffed Lobster Tail 48

Skillet Rib Eye Steaks 50

Steak With Egg & Cheese 52

Bison Meatballs 54

Keto Fried Cheese 56

Easy Slow Cooker Taco Meat 58

Chicken Liver Pate. 60

Meat-Based Meatballs 63

Easy Cucumber Sushi Recipe 65

Crusted Fish In Dijon 67

Grilled B2 Marrow With Garlic Parmesan Crust 69

Organ Meat Pie 71

Fish Sticks 73

Roasted Beef B2 Marrow 75

Trout With Butter Sauce 76

Trout With Provol2 And Pink Peppercorns 78

Keto Avocado Pie 80

Cheese Stuffed Bacon Cheeseburger 83

Cheesy Bacon Chicken 85

Easy Mediterranean Salmon Recipe 87

Easy Sizzle Fish Recipe 89

Baked Chicken Biscuit 91

Barbecued Pork Chops In The Oven 93

Herb Roasted B2 Marrow 95

Lemon Baked Cod 96

Pan Fried Salmon 98

Herb Roasted B2 Marrow 100

Chicken And Prosciutto Spiedini 101

Salmon Meatballs 103

Salmon With Caper Sauce 106

- Slow-Cooker No-Veggie Chili 108
- Carnivore Surf And Turf 110
- Spicy Keto Deviled Eggs 112
- Keto Spinach And Goat Cheese Pie 114
- Low Carb Skillet Lasagna 117
- Lemon Garlic Chicken Skewers 119
- Tortilla Pork Rind Wraps 121
- Slow-Cooker Garlicky Shrimp 123
- Easy Poached Cod In Tomato Sauce Recipe 125
- Easy Marinated Raw Fish In Coconut Cream Recipe 127
- Simple Carpaccio Beef 129
- Parmesan Baked Shrimp 131
- Seafood Creole 133
- Slow Cooker Bacon And Chicken 136
- Grilled Oysters 137
- Baked Halibut 138
- Homemade Greek Yogurt 140
- Salmon And Cream Cheese Bites 141

Cajun-Spiced Chicken Livers With Bacon And Onion

Ingredients:

- 1 pound of chicken liver pasture-raised or organic
- 1 medium-sized onion, chopped
- 6-8 slices of bacon
- 1/2 tsp of unrefined salt
- 1/2 tsp of ground black pepper
- 1/4 tsp of cayenne powder
- 1/4 tsp of garlic powder

Directions:

1. Fry the bacon in a large skillet until crispy.

2. While the bacon is baking, cut the onion and pat dry the liver with the paper towels.
3. Once the bacon is crispy, remove from the pan and let it cool. Leave the fat in the pan and add the onions and cook until tender and fragrant.
4. While the onions are baking, make a mixture of the spices.
5. NOTE: The combination of salt, pepper, cayenne and garlic mimics my all-time favorite Cajun seasoning store called Slap Ya Mama. If you prefer, add the optional paprika, oregano and thyme for the blackened Cajun seasoning. Add all the spices to a small bowl and mix well, then sprinkle evenly over all the chicken livers. Feel free to double or even triple the batch for more kick — as written, it's a soft coating. Normally, I double the seasoning.
6. When the onions have finished cooking, remove them with a slotted spoon so that you

leave as much fat in the pan as possible. If necessary, add some extra bacon fat you have a jar in your fridge, don't you?.

7. Carefully add the liver to the skillet in a single layer.
8. Cook until medium-rare, around 2-3 minutes per side.
9. Crumble the bacon in the pan and add the onions back to the pan and stir all the Ingredients: together gently. Cook for 1-2 more minutes.
10. Serve and enjoy yourself! It makes a great recipe for breakfast, lunch, or dinner.

Scotch Turkey Eggs

Ingredients:

- Cajun seasoning .5 tbsp.

- Poultry seasoning 1 tsp.

- Grain-Free Breading:

- Parmesan cheese .25 cup

- Hard-boiled eggs 6

- Ground turkey 1 lb.

- Egg regular 1

- Garlic powder 2 tsp.

- Salt & black pepper .5 tsp. each

Directions:

1. Warm the oven to reach 400° Fahrenheit. Prepare a baking tray with a layer of parchment baking paper.
2. Mix the turkey, cajun seasoning, garlic powder, and poultry seasoning.
3. Prepare six patties.
4. Whisk the egg in 2 dish and add the breading fixings in another.
5. Add the hard-boiled egg onto the patty and roll it into a ball.
6. Dip it into the egg and then the cheese mixture until covered.
7. Arrange them onto the baking sheet and set a timer for 30 minutes. Broil for 3 to 4 minutes to brown them before serving.
8. Enjoy them immediately for the best flavor results.

Lobster Tails With Animal Butter

Ingredients:

- 2 lobster tails, 3-5oz each

- ¼ tsp ground black pepper

- 1½ tbsp melted full-fat animal butter

- ¼ tsp sea salt

Directions:

1. In order to properly cut your lobster tails, point the tip of your kitchen scissor upwards through the curved edge of the top of the lobster tail when sat on a plate facing downwards.
2. Once you've cut through the shell to the tail, turn the lobster over and crack the crustacean's ribs down the center.

3. After removing the shell with your thumbs and fingers, lift the lobster meat out of the shell.
4. Word to the wise – lobster tails can be sharp, so go slowly with minimal pressure. Once you have extracted the lobster meat, cook each tail on the middle rack of your oven preheated to a strong 5 hundred-degree broil.
5. Add a cube of animal butter to each tail, and broil until the meat is at least 145°F. Cool for 10 minutes, then serve.

Keto Mushroom Omelet

Ingredients:

- 1 ounce of shredded cheese
- 3 mushrooms
- 1/5 of yellow onion
- 3 eggs
- 1 ounce of butter
- Salt and pepper

Directions:

1. Break the eggs in a mixing bowl before a pinch of salt and pepper is added. Then whisk frothy and soft with a fork.
2. Add to taste salt and spices.

3. In a frying pan, melt butter and pour in the mixture of eggs.
4. Once the omelet begins cooking and becoming firm, but for a more delightful flavour with a little raw egg on top, drizzle cheese, mushrooms, and onion on top.
5. Use a spatula to carefully alleviate the edge of the omelet before folding it in 1 . Turn off the heat and slide the omelet from the pan to a tray as quickly as it starts turning golden brown underneath.

Instant Pot Steamed Crab Legs

Ingredients:

- Lemon juice

- 2 lbs. frozen crab legs

- 4 tablespoons butter, melted

- ¾ cup water

Directions:

1. Place the steamer basket into the instant pot then put the crab legs on it.
2. Add in water and lock the lid in place.
3. Then cook for 2 minutes on high pressure then quick release.
4. The crab meat, once cooked, should be bright pink in color.
5. Combine juice with some melted butter then serve.

Spice-Rubbed Bison Tenderloin

Ingredients:

- 2 teaspoon cumin seeds, dry-toasted and ground
- 2 teaspoon coriander seeds, ground
- 1 teaspoon cinnamon
- 2 tablespoon minced garlic
- 2 sprigs fresh rosemary
- 4 six-ounce bison or beef tenderloin filets
- ½ teaspoon gray sea salt or pink rock salt
- 1 teaspoon minced fresh ginger root
- ½ teaspoon allspice

Directions:

1. Mix together ginger root, spices, garlic and rosemary in a small bowl and set aside.
2. Put the bison or beef on a 12 x 12 inch glass baking dish, and then coat both sides using the spice mix.
3. Now preheat the broiler on low and then put the fillets under it, around 6 inches from heat. Use medium low heat if using a grill pan on a stove.
4. Drizzle the meat with broth or filtered water to keep it moist.
5. This also ensures your spices don't catch fire.
6. Grill or broil for around 4 to 6 minutes until d2 , while checking the meat not to overcook it.
7. As soon as it is d2 , remove from the grill or oven and allow cool. Serve and enjoy.

Carnivore Stroganoff

Ingredients:

- ¼ cup heavy cream

- 1 tablespoon salt

- 300g ground beef

Directions:

1. Heat the oil in a pan or skillet over medium heat.
2. Slowly lay the ground meat and heat until it becomes brown.
3. Pour the heavy cream over top and season with salt.
4. Simmer it until the liquid reduces to 1 .
5. Cool it down and serve.

Carnivore Cake

Ingredients:

- 1 teaspoon vanilla extract optional

- 1 1/4 cups raw whole milk

- 5 tablespoons of cubed butter

- 4 big eggs at room temperature

- ½ cup sweetener see note optional

Directions:

1. Preheat the oven to 350 degrees Fahrenheit and assemble the Ingredients:.
2. Add eggs to the paddle attachment of a stand mixer and beat on medium-low speed for 2 to 3 minutes.
3. Add sweetener of choice and vanilla extract if using gradually while continuing to stir for 1-2 minutes.

4. In a small saucepan, boil milk and butter over medium-low heat for 3 to 4 minutes, or until the butter has melted.
5. Remove from heat and let it cool for a few minutes before proceeding.
6. Slowly blend the butter and milk combined with the egg mixture using a mixer.
7. Pour the cake batter into an 8x8 baking dish that has been buttered, and bake for 45 minutes, or until a cake tester put into the middle of the cake comes out clean.
8. Cool before serving, and savor!

Easy Almond Crusted Fish Recipe

Ingredients:

- Powdered cumin, 2 tablespoon
- Salt, to taste
- Black pepper, to taste
- Turmeric powder, 2 teaspoon
- Onion, 2 cup
- Olive oil, 3 tablespoon
- Almond flour, 4 tablespoon
- Sliced almond, 1 cup
- Smoked paprika, 1 teaspoon
- Dijon mustard, 1 cup
- Fish filet pieces, 2 pound

- Minced garlic, 3 tablespoon

- Minced ginger, 3 tablespoon

- Cilantro, 1 cup

Directions:

1. Take a large bowl.
2. Add the oil and onions into the bowl.
3. Add the chopped garlic and ginger into the bowl.
4. Add the tomatoes into the bowl.
5. Add the spices.
6. Add the cilantro into it.
7. Mix all the Ingredients: together.
8. Add the almond flour and mix your Ingredients:.
9. Cover your fish pieces with the mixture above.
10. Deep fry your fish pieces.
11. Dish them out when cooked properly.

12. Sprinkle some cilantro and sliced almond on top.
13. You can serve it with any of your preferred sauces.
14. Your dish is ready to be served.

Baked Salmon

Ingredients:

- 2 cups of lemon juice
- ½ tablespoon hot pepper
- 2 and a 1 teaspoons dried tarragon
- 1 Salmon 2 pounds fillet
- 2 tablespoons of oil, melted
- ¼ cup of white wine or chicken broth

Directions:

1. Firstly, dry out salmon. Place it in a greased 13x9-in. Baking platter. Pinch sugar.
2. Combine products leftover; spillover salmon.
3. Roast, uncovered, at 425 ° for 15-20 minutes, or quickly with a fork until the fish flakes.

Carnivore Waffles

Ingredients:

- 4 tbsp dry parmesan cheese
- 2-3 cups of water
- 10 eggs
- 8 oz ground beef
- 8 oz ground chicken or turkey

Directions:

1. Simmer the meats in 2-3 cups of water for 8-10 minutes
2. Drain in a colander and allow it to cool for 4-5 minutes
3. Preheat, the waffle maker
4. Add the parmesan and egg into the blender and blend well
5. Combine the cooked chicken and beef

6. Thoroughly blend until it is very smooth and even
7. Empty 1 the batter inside the waffle maker and then close the lid
8. Cook for 5-8 minutes or until the steam subsides
9. Repeat with the rest of the battle
10. Serve and enjoy

Carnivore Taco Pie

Ingredients:

- 1 pound ground beef

- 1 cup heavy cream

- 1 cup cheese, shredded

- 3 tablespoons taco seasoning

- 6 eggs

Directions:

1. Fore heat the oven to 350 degrees F and grease a pie pan lightly.
2. Cook the ground beef for about 5 minutes in a skillet until browned.
3. Sprinkle with taco seasoning and mix well.
4. Stir the heavy cream with eggs in a bowl and mix well.

5. Place the beef in the pie pan and top with 1 of the cheese.
6. Add the egg-cream mixture and top with the remaining cheese.
7. Shift into the oven and bake for about 30 minutes.
8. Remove from the oven and serve warm.

Vietnamese Lamb

Ingredients:

- ¼ cup sugar

- 1 tablespoon, chopped fresh chili like jalapeno

- Black pepper

- 2 pounds of lamb shoulder chops

- 1 cup chopped cilantro

- 1 cup chopped mint

- ½ cup fish sauce

- ¼ cup lime juice

Directions:

1. Combine, cilantro, mint, fish sauce, lime juice, sugar, chili like jalapeño, and black pepper.

2. Rub 1 of the mixture over 2 pounds of lamb shoulder chops or chunks, and marinate overnight.
3. Heat a grill or broiler with the rack 4 to 6 inches from the flame.
4. Wipe off the marinade; grill or broil, turning once, until medium, 4 or 5 minutes per side. Serve with the remaining sauce.

Seared Bacon Burgers

Ingredients:

- Diced bacon 4 oz.

- Ground beef 1.5 lb.

- Freshly cracked black pepper and salt .5 tsp.

Directions:

1. Dice and fry the bacon until it's crunchy.
2. Save the grease in the skillet.
3. Prepare the bacon bits and beef with pepper and salt.
4. Fry the burgers using the high setting for 8 to 10 minutes on each side.
5. Serve for brunch!

Savory Baked Chicken Thighs

Ingredients:

- 1½ tsp ground black pepper

- 1 tbsp full-fat animal fat

- 2 chicken thighs

- ½ tsp of sea salt

Directions:

1. In a clean oven-safe glass baking dish, use melted animal butter to create a non-stick layer.
2. After the dish is ready, preheat your oven to 375°F.
3. Once you have rubbed each chicken thigh thoroughly with salt and pepper, bake for thirty minutes or until the chicken juices run

clear – each thigh should reach 165°F internally before cooling.
4. Garnish with 0.25 cups of parmesan cheese for taste.

Keto Quesadillas

Ingredients:

Low-Carb Tortillas

- 1 tablespoon of coconut flour

- ½ teaspoon of salt

- 11/2 teaspoon of ground husk powder

- 2 egg white

- 2 egg

- 6 ounces of cream cheese

Filling

- 1 ounce of baby spinach

- 1 tablespoon of olive oil

- 5 ounces of grated cheese or hard cheese

Directions:

Tortillas

1. Preheat to 200 ° C your oven.
2. Whisk together the eggs and egg whites until smooth. Subsequently add the cream cheese and whisk until you have a smooth batter.
3. Combine salt, psyllium husk powder and coconut flour in a tiny bowl to be mixed properly.
4. Combine the combination of flour with the beating batter. Once correctly come, let the batter sit for a few minutes and make sure it's like a pancake batter that's dense.
5. Line a parchment paper cooking sheet and spread the batter over the parchment paper into a large square.
6. Bake on the upper rack for about 7 minutes until the tortilla turns around the edges a little brown.
7. Cut the tortilla of large size into smaller parts.

Quesadillas

1. Heat oil in a tiny skillet that is non-stick.
2. Place a piece of tortilla on top with a couple of leafy greens and even more cheese in the frying pan and drizzle cheese, before finishing with another tortilla.
3. Fry the quesadilla on both side for about a minute and it's performed and ready for consumption once the cheese melts.

Mesquite Garlic Trout

Ingredients:

- 1 teaspoon mesquite seasoning

- 2 pounds trout

- 4 tablespoons minced garlic

- 1 teaspoon salt

Directions:

1. First heat your outside grill or oven to 450 degrees F.
2. Meanwhile, cut the tail and head of a gutted and the well cleaned fish.
3. Put 4 to 5 tablespoons of minced garlic in the open belly of the fish.
4. Pour some salt and mesquite seasoning on the garlic and then wait for the trout belly to close.

5. Put the fish on an aluminum foil and loosely wrap it on the fish to fully seal it but with some air spaces.
6. Put the trout on the grill or oven and now cook for about 20 minutes.
7. As soon as the meat can easily flake, stop cooking and serve.

Beef Patties With Onion Gravy.

Ingredients:

- 4 tablespoons flour\s1 teaspoon salt\s1 tiny onion
- 1 cup chicken broth
- 500g ground beef
- 2 tablespoons butter

Directions:

1. Add seasoning Ingredients: and salt to the meat in a saucepan. Add in the flour and stir it slightly. Leave for 2 hours.
2. Make patties using the meat mixture and keep them aside.
3. Heat the pan and melt some butter in it.
4. Place all the patties and fry them on both sides.
5. Transfer to a dish.

6. Add sliced onions and broth to the pan.
7. Keep stirring until it turns into a thick gravy.
8. Pour the liquid over the patties and serve hot!

Lemon Carnivore Cheesecake

Ingredients:

- 1/2 tsp lemon extract

- 1/2 tsp vanilla extract

- 1 teaspoon fresh lemon rind OR 1 teaspoon dried lemon rind

- 2 tablespoons optional So Nourished monk fruit sweetener

- 2 cylinders of firm cream cheese 8 ounces each

- 2 eggs

- 1/4 cup sour cream

- 2 tbsp melted butter

Topping

- 3/4 cup full-fat cream

- 1/4 tsp vanilla extract

- tangy lemon zest optional

Directions:

1. Line the inside of your spring form pan with plastic wrap.
2. Prepare batter by combining all Ingredients: in a mixing bowl with an electric mixer until a smooth consistency is achieved.
3. The batter is poured into the springform pan.
4. Place a trivet I used the 2 from my InstantPot! in the bottom of the slow cooker. Or, use canning jar rings or rolled-up aluminum foil to raise the pan over the water.
5. Pour 1 cup of water into the bottom of the slow cooker.

6. Place the pan on the trivet. Cover the top of the slow cooker with paper towels to prevent water from leaking onto the cheesecake, and then cover it with the lid.
7. Cook for 2 hours on high, then turn off the slow cooker and let it rest for 1 hour.
8. Remove the cheesecake from the pan, cover it with foil or plastic wrap, and refrigerate it overnight.
9. The next day, remove the cheesecake from the pan and transfer it to a serving tray.
10. Whip the heavy cream with the vanilla extract, then spread it over the cheesecake.
11. Garnish with a touch of lemon zest optional

Instant Pot:

1. Cover the bottom and sides of the springform pan with parchment paper, unless you have a silic2 springform pan.

2. The Directions: for the cheesecake batter are the same.
3. 1 1/4 cups water should be added to the instant pot.
4. Place your trivet with lifters in the Instant pot's bottom.
5. Wrap the cake pan with aluminum foil. Place the foil-covered cake pan on the trivet and close the lid of the Instant Pot.
6. Choose the Manual mode and set the cooking duration to 30 minutes.
7. When the cooking time is complete, wait 15 minutes for the pressure to release normally. Remove the cheesecake from the oven and let it cool on the counter for 15 minutes.
8. Refrigerate the cheesecake overnight or a minimum of 4 hours.
9. Complement with unsweetened whipped cream and lemon zest optional

Easy Salt And Pepper King Fish Recipe

Ingredients:

- Minced ginger, 3 tablespoon

- Lemon juice, 1 cup

- Butter, 3 tablespoon

- Fresh herbs, 2 tablespoon

- Chopped tomatoes, 2 cup

- Onion, 2 cup

- King fish pieces, 1 pound

- Smoked paprika, 1 teaspoon

- Chopped cilantro, as required

- Minced garlic, 3 tablespoon

Directions:

1. Take a large pan.
2. Add in the butter and onions.
3. Cook the onions until they become soft and fragrant.
4. Add in the chopped garlic and ginger.
5. Cook the mixture and add the tomatoes into it.
6. Add the salt, pepper, and fresh herbs.
7. When the tomatoes are d2 , add the kingfish pieces into it.
8. Mix the Ingredients: carefully and cover your pan.
9. When d2 , dish it out.
10. Add fresh herbs on top.
11. Your dish is ready to be served.

Baked H2 Y & Spice Chicken

Ingredients:

- 1 ½ teaspoons of paprika

- Cayenne powder ¾ teaspoons

- 8 skinless, b2 less chicken breasts five ounces each

- 6 tablespoons of h2 y

- 2 tablespoons of apple vinegar

- 3 tablespoons of garlic powder

- 3 tablespoons of chili powder

- 1 ½ teaspoons of salt

- 1 ½ teaspoons of ground cumin

Directions:

1. Preheat the oven to 375 ° C., Combine six Ingredients: first; scrape over meat. Switch to a 15x10x1-in greasier. Pot baking.
2. Bake for 25-30 minutes or until 165 ° is read by a thermometer, and the juice runs free.
3. Combine the h2 y and vinegar; baste in the last 10 minutes of cooking over chicken.
4. Take it from oven and then serve it.

Carnivore Frittata

Ingredients:

- 5 eggs

- Butter, to serve

- Butter, to fry

- Nutritional yeast, optional, to serve

Directions:

1. Preheat the oven to 200 C / 390 F.
2. Beat the eggs in a bowl
3. In the oven-safe skillet, properly melt the frying butter on the stove before pouring the eggs inside
4. Move the skillet inside the oven when the top begins to bubble
5. Continue cooking for 3-5 minutes or until the top set

6. Takedown from the oven and then top up with the butter and yeast if you wish
7. Serve

Carnivore Cake

Ingredients:

- ¾ pound pork back fat, chopped
- 4 hard-boiled eggs
- 3 teaspoons Redmond Real Salt
- ½ pound pork shoulder, chopped
- 1¼ pounds pork liver, chopped

Toppings:

- 12 slices bacon
- 12 slices of prosciutto

Directions:

1. Fore heat the oven to 300 degrees F and grease a 7-inch cake pan.

2. Put the pork shoulder, pork liver, and pork back fat in a food processor and puree until smooth.
3. Put the pork mixture in the cake pan and tightly cover with foil.
4. Pour the boiling water into a roasting pan and insert the cake pan.
5. Shift into the oven and bake for about 2 hours.
6. Insert 4 egg-sized holes in the meat with a spoon and add the eggs in these holes.
7. Cover the eggs with the meat from the pan and refrigerate for 2 hours.
8. Fold the prosciutto around the cake and make bacon roses.
9. Place the bacon roses on the cake and serve to enjoy it.

Crab Stuffed Lobster Tail

Ingredients:

- 1 clove of garlic
- 1 teaspoon of fresh lemon juice
- 1 teaspoon of lemon zest
- 1 teaspoon of parsley
- ¼ teaspoon of salt
- 2 lobster tails, split along the center top
- 2 teaspoons of melted butter
- 15 buttery round crackers
- ½ a cup of jumbo lump crabmeat
- ¼ cup of butter
- 2 tablespoon of seafood seasoning

Directions:

1. Heat the oven to 220 degrees C and pull the edges of the split lobster shells apart and gently lift the tail meat to rest above the shells.
2. Place the prepared lobster tails on a baking sheet.
3. Brush each portion of tail meat with 1 teaspoon melted butter.
4. Lightly mix the crushed crackers, crabmeat, ¼ cup of clarified butter, parsley, seafood seasoning, garlic, lemon zest, lemon juice, salt, and white pepper in a bowl until thoroughly combined.
5. Spoon 1 the stuffing onto each lobster tail; press lightly to slightly shape the stuffing so it doesn't fall off.
6. Bake the lobster tails in the preheated oven until the meat is opaque and the stuffing is

golden brown on top, around 10 to 12 minutes.

Skillet Rib Eye Steaks

Ingredients:

- 2 tbsps chopped fresh rosemary leaves
- 1 tbsp unsalted butter
- 1 tbsp olive oil
- 1¼ lb b2 -in rib-eye steaks about 1¼-1½-inch thick
- 1 tsp St2 House Seasoning

Directions:

1. Rub both sides of steak with St2 House Seasoning.
2. Sprinkle with rosemary leaves.
3. Cover and refrigerate up to 3 days.

4. Remove from refrigerator and let rest at room temperature for 30 minutes.
5. Preheat a medium skillet over medium heat.
6. Add olive oil and butter and allow the butter to melt.
7. Place the steak into the skillet and cook about 5 minutes, until the bottom of the rib eye steak is caramelized and brown.
8. Turn the steak over and cook another 5 minutes, basting with the oil drippings from the skillet, until this side of the steak is also caramelized and brown.
9. Remove the steak from the heat on a cutting board and allow to rest for 5 minutes.
10. Slice against the grain when serving.

Steak With Egg & Cheese

Ingredients:

- Strip steak 8 oz.

- Eggs 1

- Bacon 2 slices if needed

Directions:

1. Either use reserved bacon grease or prepare a few slices to serve with your meal.
2. Cook the bacon in a cast-iron skillet using the medium temperature setting.
3. Leave the bacon slightly soft, and add the steak raising the temperature setting to med-high. Sear the first side of the steak and flip it over.
4. Adjust the temperature to med-low and continue cooking until it's as you like it or about five minutes.

5. Fry your egg while the steak rests. Reheat bacon if using and serve.

Bison Meatballs

Ingredients:

- 2½ tbsp non-flavored protein powder, or more for a thicker consistency

- 3 egg yolks

- 2 lb. organically sourced bison chuck

- 2 tbsp full-fat animal butter

Directions:

1. In a medium bowl, combine your bison chuck with melted animal butter, protein powder, and egg yolks.
2. While your oven preheats to 375°F, form bison meatballs that are each the size of a 2 - inch golf ball.
3. Cook your bison meatballs on an aluminum foil tray greased with animal butter for at

least twenty minutes, or until browned and crispy.

Keto Fried Cheese

Ingredients:

- ½ cup of sauce

- 1 teaspoon of dried oregano

- 20 ounces of halloumi cheese for frying

- 15 ounces of peppered red bell

Cucumber Salad

- 2 ounces of sliced cucumber

- ½ teaspoon of salt

- 2 teaspoons of dried mint

- 1/3 teaspoon of ground black pepper

- ¾ cup of mayonnaise

- 3 ounces of cream cheese

- 2 ounces of chopped pickles

Directions:

1. Through the broil function of the oven, preheat your oven to 225 ° C.
2. Using the parchment paper to line a baking sheet and arrange the peppers on it.
3. Broil until the skin starts bubbling and turns a little black.
4. Shouldn't take more than 10 to 15 minutes, but after 1 the moment, make sure to convert them.
5. Mix all the Ingredients: for the salad of the cucumber and cool.
6. Fry the cheese in olive oil for a couple of minutes on each hand.
7. Before serving, place the cheese, bell peppers and salad on the tables.

Easy Slow Cooker Taco Meat

Ingredients:

- 2 lbs. ground beef

Spices

- 1/2 teaspoon coriander
- 1 teaspoon black pepper
- 1 teaspoon sea salt
- 1 teaspoon cumin
- 1 tablespoon chili powder
- 3 tablespoons tomato paste
- 1/4 teaspoon crushed red pepper
- 1/4 teaspoon paprika
- 1/2 teaspoon onion powder

- 1/2 teaspoon garlic powder

- 1/2 teaspoon dried oregano

Directions:

1. Mix together all the spices in a small bowl.
2. Add the spices, tomato paste and the beef to the crock-pot. Mix together using a spoon.
3. Cook on low heat for 4 hours, and then break u the meat using a spoon.
4. Remove the meat from the crock-pot using a slotted spoon.

Chicken Liver Pate.

Ingredients:

- 2 cloves of garlic
- 1 tablespoon parsley
- ½ teaspoon salt\s1 shallot\s¼ teaspoon black pepper
- 500g chicken liver
- ½ cup butter

Directions:

1. Melt the butter in a pan. Sauté the garlic and shallot.
2. Fry the chicken liver in the pan on both sides until it is golden and soft. Add parsley.
3. Add the remaining butter and season with salt and pepper.

4. Stir gently to crush the Ingredients:. Pour the dish into a container and let it cool for a bit.
5. Serve with bread.
6. The carnivore diet is a high-protein weight reduction diet that contains a lot of meat, poultry, and animal products.
7. You would need to organize your day and meals around dishes that not only make you feel full but provide you with the correct nutrients and calories as per your plan.
8. The different carnivore diet dishes menti2 d here provide you with breakfast, lunch, and supper alternatives that you can simply create at home.
9. You should consider following the carnivore diet just for a short length of time since combining other meals, fruits, and vegetables will offer you a better-balanced approach towards weight reduction.

10. Make sure to visit a certified dietician before and while performing a carnivore weight reduction diet regimen.

Meat-Based Meatballs

Ingredients:

- 2 kg of meat

- 1 tbsp salt

Keto Option

- 1 big egg

- 1 tablespoon Italian Spices

- 1 teaspoon powdered garlic

- 1 teaspoon salt

- 2 kg of meat

- 1 cup mozzarella cheese shredded

- 1/2 cup grated parmesan cheese

Directions:

1. Preheat the oven to 350 degrees Fahrenheit 175 degrees Celsius.
2. In a bowl, mix the meat and salt, or combine all Ingredients: for the keto version.
3. Form 3-ounce balls in your palm.
4. Bake in a glass baking dish for 25 to 30 minutes, or until cooked and juices flow clear.
5. I use a 9-by-13-inch 23-by-33-centimeter glass dish. If you have a smaller container, put the balls very tightly.
6. It is OK for the meatballs to slightly contact when cooking.
7. Remove from oven and let cool for five minutes. Serve hot.

Easy Cucumber Sushi Recipe

Ingredients:

- Cilantro, 1 cup

- Red cabbage, 1 cup

- Green cabbage, 1 cup

- Salt, a quarter teaspoon

- Cooked rice, 2 cup

- Cream cheese, 1 cup

- Fish sauce, 2 tablespoon

- Soy sauce, a quarter cup

- Wonton wraps, as required

- Sliced cucumber, 1 cup

- Tuna cubes, 1 pound

- Ground ginger, a quarter teaspoon

- Chopped walnuts, 3 tablespoon

- Pepper, as required

Directions:

1. Cook your tuna pieces.
2. Shred your tuna pieces and place them in a bowl.
3. Mix all the Ingredients: together to form a paste.
4. Add your mixture into the wonton wrappers and wrap them up into a roll.
5. You can serve your rolls with soy sauce or fish sauce if you desire.
6. Your dish is ready to be served.

Crusted Fish In Dijon

Ingredients:

- 2 tablespoons f grated Parmesan cheese, split

- 4 filets of tilapia 5 ounces each

- ¼ cup of dried crumbs

- 2 Butter Teaspoons, cooled

- 3 tablespoons of low-fat mayonnaise

- 1 tablespoon of lemon juice

- 2 teaspoons of Dijon Mustard

- Horse radish prepared in 1 tablespoon

Directions:

1. Oven heat up to 425 ° C. Add first four items and 2 spoonful of cheese.

2. Put tilapia on a baking tray lined with melted butter; scatter thinly with a mixture of mayonnaise.
3. Apply softened butter and leftover cheese to the bread crumbs; scatter over the fillets.
4. Bake for 20 minutes, before fish only begins flaking quickly.

Grilled B2 Marrow With Garlic Parmesan Crust

Ingredients:

- Salt and pepper, to taste

- ⅓ cup olive oil

- ¼ cup parmesan cheese, grated

- ½ cup parsley, chopped

- 4 beef marrow b2 s, cut lengthwise

- 4 garlic cloves, minced

Directions:

1. Fore heat the grill to medium-high and grease the grill grates.
2. Combine garlic, parsley, olive oil, salt, and pepper in a bowl.
3. Decant this mixture over the top of the beef marrow b2 s and top with parmesan cheese.

4. Transfer to the grill and cook for about 10 minutes.
5. Remove from the grill and serve hot.

Organ Meat Pie

Ingredients:

- ½ pound ground beef liver

- 3 eggs

- 2 tablespoons beef tallow

- ½ pound ground beef heart

- ½ pound ground beef

- Salt, to taste

Directions:

1. Fore heat the oven to 350 degrees F and grease a 9-inch pie plate.
2. Combine ground beef with the rest of the Ingredients: in a bowl.
3. Decant the beef mixture into the pie plate and transfer it in the oven.

4. Bake for about 20 minutes and remove from the oven to serve.

Fish Sticks

Ingredients:

- ½ a teaspoon of lemon pepper seasoning

- ½ a cup of all-purpose almond ground flax meal

- 1 large egg beaten

- ¾ pound of cod fillets cut into 1 inch strips

- ½ a cup of dried almond meal

- ½ a teaspoon of salt

- ½ a teaspoon of paprika

Directions:

1. Preheat the oven to 400 degrees. In a shallow bowl, mix almond meal and seasonings then place the almond ground flax meal and egg in another bowl.

2. Dip the fish in the almond ground flax meal and coat both sides when d2 shake off the excess.
3. Dip it in the egg then in the crumb mixture and pat it to make sure it sticks properly.
4. Place it on a piece of aluminum foil in a baking tray coated with butter.
5. Bake until the fish starts to flake and turn over. Do the same to the other side and serve.

Roasted Beef B2 Marrow

Ingredients:

- 4 beef b2 marrow halves

- A Pinch sea salt

Directions:

1. Preheat oven to 350° F.
2. Place the b2 s on a baking tray; marrow side facing up.
3. Bake for 20-30 minutes until the b2 and marrow are golden.

Trout With Butter Sauce

Ingredients:

- Fresh chives: 3 Tbsp. [chopped].

- Butter: 6 Tbsp.

- Olive oil: 2 Tbsp.

- Lemon juice: 2 tsp.

- Trout fillets: 4

- Salt and ground black pepper to taste

- Lemon zest: 3 tsp. [grated].

Directions:

1. Season trout with salt, pepper, and drizzle olive oil. Massage into fish.
2. Heat a kitchen grill over medium heat.
3. Add fish fillets and cook for 4 minutes. Flip and cook for another 4 minutes.

4. Heat butter in a pan.
5. Add lemon juice, lemon zest, chives, salt, and pepper. Mix well.
6. Divide fish fillets on plates.
7. Drizzle with the butter sauce and serve.

Trout With Provol2 And Pink Peppercorns

Ingredients:

- ¼ tsp ground pink peppercorns

- 1 tbsp full-fat animal butter

- 4oz fillet of wild-caught trout

- ½ cup shredded provol2 cheese

Directions:

1. In a medium skillet over melted full-fat animal butter, cook your trout piece skin-down for at least twenty minutes until the fish on top is flaky.
2. Once you have achieved your desired consistency, remove the trout from the heat and season with sea salt and ground pink peppercorns.

3. Garnish with shredded provol2 cheese and rest for 2 minutes before serving. Be sure to avoid ingesting the skin.

Keto Avocado Pie

Ingredients:

Pie Crust

- 1 tablespoon of ground husk powder

- Pinch of salt

- 1 egg

- 3 tablespoons of olive oil

- 4 tablespoons of water

- 4 tablespoons of sesame seeds

- 4 tablespoons of coconut flour

- ¾ cup of almond flour

- 1 teaspoon of baking powder

Filling

- ½ cup of cream cheese

- 1 cup of mayonnaise

- cups of heavy cream

- 1 finely chopped red chili pepper

- 2 ripe avocados

- 3 eggs

- 2 tablespoons of finely sliced fresh cilantro

- ½ teaspoon of onion powder

Directions:

1. Preheat to 175 ° C on the oven.
2. Mix all the comp2 nts for the pie dough in a food processor for a few minutes until the dough looks like a ball. Alternatively, you can use either your hands or a fork to knead the Ingredients: together in a bowl.
3. Line a 12-inch parchment paper pan and grease the pan as well as the paper.

4. Use an oiled spatula or fingers to spread dough into the pan before pre-baking the crust for 10–15 minutes.
5. Split the avocado and dice; remove the seeds from the chili while chopping the chili finely before putting it in a bowl with the avocado to mix with the other comp2 nts.
6. Pour the entire blend into the pie crust until lightly golden brown for 35 minutes in the oven.
7. Allow a few minutes to cool down and serve with a green salad.

Cheese Stuffed Bacon Cheeseburger

Ingredients:

- 2 oz. cheddar cheese

- 1 oz. mozzarella cheese

- 2 slices bacon, pre-cooked

- 8 oz. ground beef

- 1 tablespoon butter

- 1 teaspoon Cajun seasoning

- 1/2 teaspoon pepper

- 1 teaspoon salt

Directions:

1. Use all spices to season the ground beef and mix together lightly.

2. Cube the mozzarella cheese and slice the cheddar.
3. Now grab the seas2 d ground beef, and make rough patties from it.
4. Once d2 , put the mozzarella inside and now enclose the cheese with the beef.
5. In a pan, heat a tablespoon of butter until bubbling and hot. Add 2 burger to the hot pan.
6. Cover using a cloche and cook for 2-3 minutes.
7. Then flip the burger and put the cheddar on top.
8. Cover the pan with cloche again and cook for 1-2 minutes.
9. Finally chop bacon slice in 1 and put it over the burger. Serve.

Cheesy Bacon Chicken

Ingredients:

- 2 tablespoons seasoning rub

- 5-6 chicken breasts, cut in 1 width wise

- Barbecue sauce, optional

- 4 ounce shredded cheddar

- 1/2 pound bacon, cut strips in 1

Directions:

1. Heat the oven to 400 degrees F. Meanwhile, coat a baking sheet that is rimmed with cooking spray.
2. With the season rub, season both sides of chicken and top each breast with bacon.
3. Bake the chicken until it looks crispy and the meat thermometer indicates 160 degrees, or for approximately 30 minutes.

4. Then remove from the hot oven and distribute the cheese over bacon strips.
5. Return to the oven and now bake until the cheese is bubbly and golden, or for another 10 minutes.
6. Serve the cheesy bacon chicken with barbeque sauce if you like.

Easy Mediterranean Salmon Recipe

Ingredients:

- Minced garlic, 3 tablespoon

- Minced ginger, 3 tablespoon

- Lemon juice, 1 cup

- Butter, 3 tablespoon

- Fresh herbs, 2 tablespoon

- Chopped tomatoes, 2 cup

- Mediterranean red sauce, 2 cup

- Mediterranean spice, 2 teaspoon

- Onion, 2 cup

- Salmon pieces, 1 pound

- Smoked paprika, 1 teaspoon

- Chopped cilantro, as required

Directions:

1. Take a large pan.
2. Add in the butter and onions.
3. Cook the onions until they become soft and fragrant.
4. Add in the chopped garlic and ginger.
5. Cook the mixture and add the tomatoes into it.
6. Add the spices and fresh herbs.
7. When the tomatoes are d2 , add the salmon pieces and Mediterranean red sauce into it.
8. Mix the Ingredients: carefully and cover your pan.
9. When d2 , dish it out.
10. Add the cilantro on top.
11. Your dish is ready to be served.

Easy Sizzle Fish Recipe

Ingredients:

- Fish filet pieces, 2 pound
- Minced garlic, 3 tablespoon
- Minced ginger, 3 tablespoon
- Cilantro, 1 cup
- Olive oil, 3 tablespoon
- Powdered cumin, 2 tablespoon
- Salt, to taste
- Black pepper, to taste
- Turmeric powder, 2 teaspoon
- Onion, 2 cup
- Smoked paprika, 1 teaspoon

Directions:

1. Take a large bowl.
2. Add the oil and onions into the bowl.
3. Add the chopped garlic and ginger into the bowl.
4. Add the tomatoes into the bowl.
5. Add the spices.
6. Add the cilantro into it.
7. Mix all the Ingredients: together.
8. Cover your fish pieces with the mixture above.
9. Grill your fish pieces.
10. Dish them out when cooked properly.
11. Sprinkle some cilantro on top.
12. You can serve it with any of your preferred sauces.
13. Your dish is ready to be served.

Baked Chicken Biscuit

Ingredients:

- ¼ tablespoon dry thyme

- 1 cup cookie/baking blend

- ½ cup of whole milk

- 1 big egg

- 1 cup of dried, thawed mixed vegetables

- 1 ½ tables of fried chicken

- 1 can condensed chicken soup cream

Directions:

1. Mix tomatoes, meat, broth and thyme in a big saucepan.
2. Spill into an unbuttered 9-in deep-dish. Piece of a pie.

3. Merge a mixture of cookies, milk and egg; pour over a mixture of meat.
4. Bake at 400 ° for 25-30 minutes, until lightly browned.

Barbecued Pork Chops In The Oven

Ingredients:

- ½ tablespoon hot pepper

- ½ teaspoon chili powder

- ½ teaspoon of paprika

- Ketchup: 3/4 cup

- 1/3 cup of warm water

- 6 b2 -in loin pork chops 3/4 "thick

- 1 spoonful of Worcestershire sauce

- 2 cups of vinegar

- 2 tablespoons of brown sugar

Directions:

1. Position the chops in wide cast iron or other oven tray skillet, slightly overlapping where possible.
2. Combine products leftover; spillover beef.
3. Bake for 40 minutes, uncovered, at 375 °, rotating chops midway during preparation.

Herb Roasted B2 Marrow

Ingredients:

- 2 beef marrow b2 s, grass-fed/pasture-raised

- 1 tablespoon fresh thyme

- 1 tablespoon fresh rosemary

- Salt and black pepper, to taste

Directions:

1. Fore heat the oven to 400 degrees F and grease a baking dish.
2. Arrange the b2 marrows on the baking dish and season with salt, pepper, thyme, and rosemary.
3. Shift into the oven and bake for about 15 minutes.
4. Dish out in a platter and serve warm.

Lemon Baked Cod

Ingredients:

- ¼ teaspoon paprika

- 4 cod fillets 6 ounces each

- 2 teaspoons grated lemon zest

- ¼ teaspoon of crushed garlic

- 3 tablespoons of lemon juice

- 3 tablespoons of melted butter

- ¼ cup all-purpose almond ground flax meal

- ½ teaspoon salt

Directions:

1. Preheat the oven to 400 degrees F and rub a baking sheet with melted butter.

2. Add the rest of the butter, the lemon juice, garlic, salt and pepper in a small bowl and mix together until well combined.
3. Spread the butter mixture evenly over each piece of salmon and bake for about 15-20 minutes or when the cod is opaque and easily flakes when turned over with a fork.

Pan Fried Salmon

Ingredients:

- ½ teaspoon of garlic powder

- ½ teaspoon dried rosemary

- 2 tablespoons of unsalted butter

- 2 salmon fillets, B2 s removed, skin on

- ½ teaspoon of salt

- ¼ teaspoon of black pepper

Directions:

1. Dry the salmon fillets with paper towels. Sprinkle them with the salt, pepper, and garlic powder.
2. Heat the butter in a large nonstick pan over medium-high heat, about 2 minutes.
3. Add the salmon fillets, skin side down.

4. Cook until skin is browned and crisp, about 3 minutes.
5. Use a spatula to carefully turn the fillets.
6. Cook until browned on the second side and cooked through, after 2-3 more minutes.
7. Transfer the salmon to plates and pour the butter from the pan on top. Serve immediately.

Herb Roasted B2 Marrow

Ingredients:

- ¼ tsp fresh thyme, chopped
- Salt and black pepper, to taste
- 4 marrow beef b2 s
- ¼ tsp fresh rosemary, chopped

Directions:

1. Preheat the oven to 400° F.
2. Place the b2 s in a baking dish and sprinkle with rosemary and thyme.
3. Roast for about 15 minutes, until no longer pink inside.
4. Season with salt and pepper.
5. Serve hot.

Chicken And Prosciutto Spiedini

Ingredients:

- ½ tsp kosher salt

- ⅛ tsp ground black pepper

- 16 fresh basil leaves

- ¼ tsp garlic powder

- 8 skewers

- 8 raw chicken tenders

- 8 oz block provol2 cheese

- 8 slices prosciutto

Directions:

1. Combine the garlic powder, kosher salt, and pepper.

2. Trim the chicken tenders of the tendons, and then pound them out to a 1-inch thickness.
3. Season the chicken with the spice mixture.
4. Cut the provol2 cheese into pieces about 1-2 inches long.
5. On a cutting board, place a slice of prosciutto.
6. Then top with a chicken tender and 3 leaves of fresh basil. Next place a piece of cheese across the basil.
7. Carefully roll the bundle and skewer it.
8. Preheat a grill to 325-375°F. Grill for about 3-5 minutes per side, or until a thermometer reads 165°F in the center and the skewers are cooked through.
9. Serve warm.

Salmon Meatballs

Ingredients:

- Fresh chives: ¼ cup [chopped].

- Egg: 1

- Dijon mustard - 2 Tbsp.

- Coconut flour: 1 Tbsp.

- Salt and ground black pepper to taste

- Butter: 2 Tbsp.

- Garlic cloves: 2 [minced].

- Onion: 1/3 cup [chopped].

- Wild salmon: 1 pound [b2 less and minced].

For The Sauce:

- Juice and zest of 1 lemon

- Coconut cream: 2 cups
- Fresh chives: 2 Tbsp. [chopped].
- Garlic: 4 cloves [minced].
- Butter: 2 Tbsp.
- Dijon mustard: 2 Tbsp.

Directions:

1. Heat 2 tbsp. butter in a pan.
2. Add onion and 2 garlic cloves.
3. Stir-fry for 3 minutes and transfer to a bowl.
4. In another bowl, mix the onion and garlic with salmon, egg, 2 tbsp. mustard, salt, pepper, coconut flour, and chives.
5. Shape meatballs from the salmon mixture and place on a baking sheet.
6. Bake at 350F for 25 minutes.
7. Heat a pan with 2 tbsp. butter over medium heat.

8. Add 4 garlic cloves. Stir-fry for 1 minute.
9. Add chives, lemon juice, lemon zest, 2 tbsp. Dijon mustard, and coconut cream. Cook for 3 minutes.
10. Take salmon meatballs out of the oven; drop them into the Dijon sauce. Toss and cook for 1 minute.
11. Serve.

Salmon With Caper Sauce

Ingredients:

- Capers: 2 Tbsp.

- Lemon juice: 3 Tbsp.

- Garlic: 4 cloves [minced].

- Butter: 2 Tbsp.

- Salmon fillets - 3

- Salt and ground black pepper to taste

- Olive oil: 1 Tbsp.

- Italian seasoning: 1 Tbsp.

Directions:

1. Heat olive oil in a pan over medium heat.
2. Add fish fillets skin side up. Season with salt, pepper, and seasoning.

3. Cook for 2 minutes, flip and cook for 2 minutes again.
4. Remove from the heat, cover pan, and set aside for 15 minutes.
5. Transfer fish to a plate, and leave them aside.
6. Heat the same pan over medium heat.
7. Add capers, lemon juice, and garlic. Stir-fry for 2 minutes.
8. Take the pan off the heat and butter and stir well.
9. Return fish to the pan and toss to coat with the sauce.
10. Serve.

Slow-Cooker No-Veggie Chili

Ingredients:

- 8-10 cups of b2 broth

- 1 cup mozzarella cheese

- ½ cup yellow cheddar cheese

- Sea salt and black pepper to preference

- 2oz chicken breast, cooked and shredded

- ½ lb. ground beef

- ½ lb. ground turkey

- 2 cups cubed pork belly

Directions:

1. To make your b2 broth, boil together with the b2 s, connective tissues, and marrow of either chicken, pork, beef, or all 4 , simmering for

more than 24 hours if your mixture includes more red meat b2 s than chicken b2 s, but only 24 hours if you chose to cook only chicken.
2. After a maximum of forty-eight hours, strain your broth. In a large slow cooker set to medium, add in your b2 broth, turkey, pork belly, chicken, and your cheeses.
3. Leave to cook for at least 6 hours, stirring if you can.
4. After 6 hours, let cool and garnish with parmesan cheese.

Carnivore Surf And Turf

Ingredients:

- ¼ tsp of sea salt

- 4oz filet mignon steak

- 10 – 12 large prawns, peeled and veined

- 1 tbsp melted full-fat animal butter

- ¼ tsp fresh ground pepper

Directions:

1. In a large bowl, combine all your shrimp with the sea salt and pepper and then cover to refrigerate for at least fifteen minutes.
2. With your grill turned up to medium or high heat depending on your personal preference, cook your steak until as tough or tender as you wish.

3. Once your steak has finished, cook your shrimp either on skewers or in an aluminum foil boat until pink but not solidly white.
4. Dress with more sea salt and pepper to taste.

Spicy Keto Deviled Eggs

Ingredients:

- 1/3 teaspoon of salt

- 1/2 tablespoon of poppy seeds

- 6 eggs

- 1 tablespoon of red curry paste

Directions:

1. Boil the eggs without a cap in a pan that contains water.
2. Allow the eggs to cook for approximately eight minutes and enable ice-cold water to cool rapidly.
3. Remove the shells of the egg; cut the 3 ends off and divide the egg into 3 . Excavate the yolk of the egg and place it in a tiny bowl.
4. Place the white eggs on a tray and cool.

5. Combine a soft batter with curry paste, mayonnaise, and egg yolks; then add salt to taste.
6. Remove from the fridge the egg whites and add the batter.
7. Sprinkle and serve the seeds over it.

Keto Spinach And Goat Cheese Pie

Ingredients:

Pie Crust:

- 11/2 ounces of butter

- 1 egg

- 1 tablespoon of ground husk powder

- 11/3 cups of almond floor

- 31/3 tablespoons of sesame seed

- ½ teaspoon of salt

Egg Batter:

- Salt and pepper

- 1 cup of heavy sour cream

- 5 eggs

Spinach And Goat Cheese Filling:

- 2 tablespoons of coconut oil

- A pinch of ground nutmeg

- 6 ounces of sliced goat cheese

- 2 cloves of garlic

- Salt and pepper

- 7 ounces of fresh spinach

Directions:

1. Preheat to 170 ° C on the oven.
2. Before adding the remaining Ingredients:, combine almond flour and sesame seeds together in a blender and blend well to create a dough. Press the dough into a springform pan and insert holes into it using a fork.
3. Pie shell pre-baked for 10-15 minutes.

4. Before adding salt and pepper, whisk together the eggs and whipping cream.
5. Cut the spinach tightly and finely slice the garlic. In butter or oil, sauté the garlic, put in the spinach, then season.
6. Add the spinach sautéed to the shell of the pre-baked pie.
7. Mix the rubbed cheese in the batter of the eggs and pour over it the spinach before overlapping with goat cheese.
8. Bake for 30–40 minutes in the oven at 175 ° C.

Low Carb Skillet Lasagna

Ingredients:

- 24 ounce jar no sugar added marinara sauce

- 2 teaspoons fine sea salt

- 1 pound 80% lean ground beef

- 1 teaspoon fresh oregano, chopped

- 1 cup shredded mozzarella cheese divided, about 4 ounces

- 4 slices thin roast chicken breast from deli counter

Directions:

1. Brown the beef in a 10 inch cast iron skillet over medium high heat, while seasoning the meat with sea salt as it cooks.

2. Cook the beef for around 5 minutes or until cooked through. Keep breaking up the beef using a spatula as it cooks.
3. Add in the sauce, stir to blend then push 1 of the cooked beef off 2 side of the skillet.
4. Now put a layer of sliced chicken breast on the bottom of the cooking pan and top the meat with 1 cup of shredded cheese.
5. Then scoop the beef on top of left over bacon to create an even layer. Top with the reserved 1/2 cup of cheese and sprinkle with some oregano.
6. Cover the mixture and heat on low to fully melt the cheese.

Lemon Garlic Chicken Skewers

Ingredients:

- 3/4 cup Tessemae's Lemon Garlic

- 4 chicken breasts, cut into 1 inch cubes

- 2 tablespoon fresh parsley, chopped

Directions:

1. To a bowl or zip lock bag, add the lemon garlic dressing and chicken and let coat for a few minutes.
2. Keep it chilled for 1 to 3 hours.
3. Meanwhile, preheat the grill to around 500 degrees F and then start treading the chicken onto the skewers.
4. If using wooden skewers, soak them in water about 30 minutes before use.
5. Once the grill is hot enough, put the skewers on the grill and cook until the chicken is well

cooked, while flipping 1 way through to enable even cooking.

6. After about 15 minutes or so, remove from the grill and garnish with fresh herbs such as parsley or others.

7. You can also cook the chicken under a broiler or a grill pan and ensure the internal temperature reaches 160 degrees before serving.

Tortilla Pork Rind Wraps

Ingredients:

- 1/2 teaspoon garlic powder

- 3 ounces pork rinds, crushed

- 4 large eggs

- 1/4 teaspoon ground cumin

- Butter

Directions:

1. Mix together eggs, garlic powder, pork rinds and cumin in a food processor or blender until well combined and smooth.
2. Add about ¼ cups of water, and continue blending; and add more water as required to achieve pancake batter consistency.
3. Now over medium-low heat, melt 1 teaspoon of coconut or avocado oil in a non-stick skillet.

4. Swirl to coat the pan, and then add around 3 tablespoons of batter. Spread it thinly over the pan using a rubber spatula, almost to edges.
5. Cook the batter until the bottom starts to brown, or for approximately 1 minute.
6. With a spoon, carefully loosen the edges and flip the pancake. Cook the other side for approximately 1 minute.
7. Repeat steps 2 and 3 with the rest of the batter, but only add oil to the skillet if required. You need less oil in the pan to easily spread batter.
8. Continue adding water to the batter as required throughout cooking as it may thicken with time.
9. Serve when d2 with the cooking.

Slow-Cooker Garlicky Shrimp

Ingredients:

- 1/4 teaspoon black pepper, freshly ground
- 1 teaspoon kosher salt
- 1 teaspoon smoked Spanish paprika
- 6 cloves garlic, thinly sliced
- 3/4 cup melted butter
- 1 tablespoon flat-leaf parsley, minced
- 2 pounds extra-large raw shrimp, peeled and deveined
- 1/4 teaspoon crushed red pepper flakes

Directions:

1. Mix together crushed pepper flakes, black pepper, salt, paprika, garlic and oil in a crock pot. Stir the mixture to incorporate.
2. Then cover and cook for 30 minutes on high heat settings.
3. Now stir in shrimp to coat it then cover and cook for another 10 minutes.
4. Stir to help the shrimp cook evenly until all of the fish meat is opaque or for about 10 minutes or so.
5. Move the fish and its sauce to a serving dish then sprinkles with parsley to garnish. Serve it warm.

Easy Poached Cod In Tomato Sauce Recipe

Ingredients:

- Red chili powder, 2 teaspoon

- Cilantro, 1 cup

- Salt, a quarter teaspoon

- Red chili paste, 2 tablespoon

- Greek yoghurt, as required

- Peanuts, 1 cup

- Cod cubes, 1 pound

- Ground ginger, a quarter teaspoon

- Pecan pieces, 3 tablespoon

- Tomato paste, 2 cup

- Pepper, as required

Directions:

1. Boil the cod cubes.
2. In a large pan, add all the Ingredients: except the cod pieces.
3. Cook your tomato sauce.
4. Add the cod pieces and let them simmer for five to ten minutes.
5. Add peanuts and Greek yoghurt on top.
6. Your dish is ready to be served.

Easy Marinated Raw Fish In Coconut Cream Recipe

Ingredients:

- Raw fish pieces, 1 pound

- Maple syrup, 2 teaspoon

- Ground ginger, a quarter teaspoon

- Pecan pieces, 3 tablespoon

- Lemon juice, 1 cup

- Pepper, as required

- Cilantro, 1 cup

- Salt, a quarter teaspoon

- Red chili paste, 2 tablespoon

- Coconut cream, a quarter cup

- Shredded coconut flakes, as required

- Chopped chives, 1 cup

Directions:

1. Clean your raw fish pieces.
2. Mix all the Ingredients: along with the fish pieces.
3. Add in the lemon juice and other spices.
4. Add in the fish pieces.
5. Drain off the excess marinade.
6. Add cilantro leaves on top.
7. Your dish is ready to be served.

Simple Carpaccio Beef

Ingredients:

- 2 tablespoons of toasted pine nuts
- 2 teaspoons of chives, finely minced
- ½ cup 40 g of parmesan rasped
- 250 g beef fillet in highest condition, trimmed
- 2 teaspoons of truffle oil or extra virgin olive oil

Directions:

1. Place the beef in aluminum foil securely and chill for 30 minutes this should make it easier to cut finely.
2. Unpack the beef, using a razor blade, and cut very evenly.
3. Put the beef slices inside plastic cover sheets, and straighten them with a wooden spoon.

4. Place 4 or 5 slices of beef aside on every large dish and sprinkle it with oil.
5. Rub it well with salt from the sea and freshly roasted black pepper, then sprinkle with pine nuts, chives and parmesan rind.
6. Serve with lemon wedges and rocket seeds.

Parmesan Baked Shrimp

Ingredients:

- ½ teaspoon black pepper

- 1 teaspoon garlic powder

- 24 oz. jumbo shrimp peeled and deveined, patted dry

- ½ teaspoon paprika

- 4 tablespoons butter

- Cup grated Parmesan

- Avocado oil cooking spray

Directions:

1. Preheat oven to 233 degrees C. Line a rimmed baking sheet with parchment paper.
2. Place the butter in a shallow microwave safe bowl. Melt in the microwave.

3. In another medium bowl, whisk together the Parmesan, black pepper and garlic powder.
4. Divide the mixture into 3 separate shallow bowls – this will ensure the Parmesan stays as dry as possible, making it easier to coat the shrimp.
5. Dip each shrimp in the melted butter to coat, then roll in the Parmesan mixture.
6. Arrange the coated shrimp in a single layer on the prepared baking sheet.
7. Sprinkle them with paprika and spray with avocado oil.
8. Bake the Parmesan shrimp until cooked through, about 10 minutes and serve immediately.

Seafood Creole

Ingredients:

- ½ a cup of peeled chopped onion
- ¾ cup of chopped onion
- ¾ cup of chopped celery
- ¾ cup of chopped green bell peppers
- ½ teaspoon of minced garlic
- 1 ¼ cup of chicken stock
- 1 cup of canned tomato sauce
- 1 teaspoon of white sugar
- ½ teaspoon of hot pepper sauce
- Bay leaves
- 1 pound of peeled and deveined shrimp

- 1 pound of scallops
- 1 pound of haddock fillets
- ¾ teaspoon of dried oregano
- ½ teaspoon of salt
- ½ teaspoon of ground white pepper
- ½ teaspoon of ground black pepper
- ½ teaspoon of cayenne pepper
- ½ teaspoon of dried thyme leaves
- ½ teaspoon of dried sweet basil
- ¼ a cup of butter

Directions:

1. Mix together oregano, salt, white pepper, black pepper, cayenne pepper, thyme, and basil in a small bowl; set aside.

2. Melt butter in a large oven over medium heat; stir in tomato, onion, celery, green bell pepper, and garlic.
3. Cook and stir until the onion is translucent, about 5 minutes.
4. Stir in chicken stock, tomato sauce, sugar, hot pepper sauce, and bay leaves.
5. Reduce heat to low and bring sauce to a simmer.
6. Stir in seasoning mix and simmer until the flavors have blended, about 20 minutes.
7. Gently stir in shrimp, scallops, and haddock; bring sauce back to a simmer and cook until the shellfish and fish are opaque, about 20 more minutes. Remove bay leaves to serve.

Slow Cooker Bacon And Chicken

Ingredients:

- 1 tbsp oregano, dried

- 1 tbsp rosemary, dried

- 5 tbsp olive oil, divided

- 1 tbsp salt

- 5 chicken breasts

- 10 slices bacon

- 2 tbsp thyme, dried

Directions:

1. Into a slow cooker pot, combine all the Ingredients: and 3 tablespoons of olive oil.
2. Cook on low for 8 hours.
3. Shred the meat and mix with remaining olive oil.

Grilled Oysters

Ingredients:

- Lemon: 1 [cut in wedges].

- Parsley: 1 Tbsp.

- Sweet paprika: 1 pinch

- Melted butter: 2 Tbsp.

- Oysters: 6 [shucked].

- Garlic: 3 cloves [peeled and minced].

Directions:

1. Top each oyster with melted butter, parsley, and paprika.
2. Place on a preheated grill pan over medium-high heat, and cook for 8 minutes.
3. Serve them with lemon wedges on the side.

Baked Halibut

Ingredients:

- Garlic: 6 cloves [minced].

- Tabasco sauce: 1 dash

- Halibut fillets: 4

- Salt and ground black pepper to taste

- Juice of ½ lemon

- Parmesan cheese: ½ cup [grated].

- Butter: ¼ cup

- Mayonnaise: ¼ cup

- Green onions: 2 Tbsp. [chopped].

Directions:

1. Season halibut with salt, pepper, and some of the lemon juice.

2. Place in the baking dish, and cook in the oven at 450F for 6 minutes.
3. Heat butter in a pan.
4. Add parmesan cheese, mayonnaise, green onions, Tabasco sauce, garlic, remaining lemon juice, and mix well.
5. Take fish out of the oven and drizzle cheese sauce all over.
6. Turn the oven to broil and broil the fish for 3 minutes.
7. Serve.

Homemade Greek Yogurt

Ingredients:

- ½ cup plain full-fat yogurt

- ½ gallon whole milk

Directions:

1. To make Greek yoghurt, line a fine mesh using 3 layers of cheesecloth, then put it in a large bowl.
2. Move the yoghurt to a sieve and allow the liquid whey to drain so that you can get preferred yoghurt consistency.
3. This should take around 4 hours.
4. Chill the yoghurt and then serve.

Salmon And Cream Cheese Bites

Ingredients:

- 50 g shredded/grated cheese

- 1/2 teaspoon salt

- 250 ml cow/goat milk

- 6 medium sized eggs

- 50 grams cream cheese

- 1 teaspoon dried dill

- 50 g fresh or smoked salmon slices

Directions:

1. In a large pouring jug, whisk together eggs, coconut milk and salt and then fold in dill, smoked salmon, grated cheese and chopped cream cheese.

2. Pour the batter into greased silicon molds or mini muffin trays.
3. Bake the mixture at about 180 degrees C for about 10 to 15 minutes.
4. Allow to cool and then serve.

www.ingramcontent.com/pod-product-compliance
Lightning Source LLC
LaVergne TN
LVHW011946070526
838202LV00054B/4823